THE PENGUIN POETS

THE LONG APPROACH

Maxine Kumin, who won the Pulitzer Prize in 1973 and was Consultant in Poetry to the Library of Congress for 1981–82, was born in Philadelphia, educated at Radcliffe College, and now lives in Warner, New Hampshire. The author of four novels, seven volumes of poetry, a collection of critical essays, and a short fiction collection, she has taught at Washington University, Brandeis, Columbia, Princeton, and elsewhere. In 1986 she was awarded the Academy of American Poets' prize "for distinguished poetic achievement."

Also by Maxine Kumin

POETRY

Halfway
The Privilege
The Nightmare Factory
Up Country: Poems of New England
House, Bridge, Fountain, Gate
The Retrieval System
Our Ground Time Here Will Be Brief

FICTION

Through Dooms of Love
The Passions of Uxport
The Abduction
The Designated Heir
Why Can't We Live Together Like
    Civilized Human Beings?

ESSAYS

To Make a Prairie: Essays on Poets,
    Poetry, and Country Living

THE

LONG

APPROACH

Poems by

Maxine Kumin

VIKING
PENGUIN BOOKS

PENGUIN BOOKS
Viking Penguin Inc., 40 West 23rd Street,
New York, New York 10010, U.S.A.
Penguin Books Ltd, Harmondsworth,
Middlesex, England
Penguin Books Australia Ltd, Ringwood,
Victoria, Australia
Penguin Books Canada Limited, 2801 John Street,
Markham, Ontario, Canada L3R 1B4
Penguin Books (N.Z.) Ltd, 182–190 Wairau Road,
Auckland 10, New Zealand

First published in the United States of America by
Viking Penguin Inc. 1985
Published in Penguin Books 1986

Page ix constitutes an extension of this copyright page.

LIBRARY OF CONGRESS CATALOGING IN PUBLICATION DATA
Kumin, Maxine, 1925–
The long approach.
(Penguin poets)
I. Title.
[PS3521.U638L6   1986]   811'.54   86-4955
ISBN   0-670-80429-0 (cloth)
0 14 042.342 7 (paperback)

Printed in the United States of America by
R. R. Donnelley & Sons Company, Harrisonburg, Virginia
Set in Melior

again, for Victor

CONTENTS

III. ON THE FARM

Some of the poems in this book were previously published as follows: "You Are in Bear Country" and "Appetite" in *American Poetry Review*; "Louise Bourgeois Exhibit" in *The Bennington Review*; "In the Upper Pasture" in *Blair & Ketchum's Country Journal*; "Strut" in *Breeders' Cup Magazine*; "Introducing the Fathers" and "Diary" in *Crazy Horse*; "Expatriate" and "Out in It" in *Embers*; "The Chain" in *Memphis State Review*; "Video Cuisine" and "Atlantic City 1939" in *The Nation*; "Shelling Jacobs Cattle Beans" in *New England Review/Bread Loaf Quarterly*; "At a Private Showing in 1982" in *The New Yorker*; "After the Harvest" and "The Long Approach" in *Ontario Review*; "Waiting for the End in New Smyrna Beach, Florida" and "Caring: A Dream" in *Parnassus*; "How to Survive Nuclear War" in *Ploughshares*; "Grandchild" and "Sundays in March" in *Poetry*; "Getting Through" in *Science 85*; "The Poet Visits Egypt and Israel" in *Southern Poetry Review*; "Visiting Professor" and "In the Absence of Bliss" in *Tendril*; "Shopping in Ferney with Voltaire" in *TriQuarterly*; and "Gladly" in *Whales: A Celebration*, edited by Greg Gatenby, Little, Brown, 1983. "At a Private Showing in 1982" was reprinted in *Singular Voices: American Poetry Today*, edited by Stephen Berg, Avon Books, 1985.

I looked with awe at the ground I trod on, to see what the Powers had made there, the form and fashion and material of their work. This was that Earth of which we have heard, made out of Chaos and Old Night. Here was no man's garden, but the unhandselled globe. It was not lawn, nor pasture, nor mead, nor woodland, nor lea, nor arable, nor waste-land. It was the fresh and natural surface of the planet Earth, as it was made for ever and ever—to be the dwelling of man, we say—so Nature made it, and man may use it if he can.

—Henry David Thoreau, *The Maine Woods*

Prologue

YOU ARE IN BEAR COUNTRY

Advice from a pamphlet published by the
Canadian Minister of the Environment

They've
been here
for thousands of years.
You're
the visitor.
Avoid
encounters. Think ahead.
Keep clear
of berry patches
garbage dumps, carcasses.
On woods walks bring
noisemakers, bells.
Clap hands along the trail
or sing
but in dense bush
or by running water
bear may not hear your clatter.
Whatever else
don't whistle. Whistling
is thought by some to imitate
the sounds bears make when they mate.

You need to know
there are two kinds:
ursus arctus horribilis
or grizzly

and ursus *americanus*
the smaller black
said to be
somewhat less likely to attack.
Alas, a small *horribilis*
is difficult to distinguish
from a large *americanus*.

Although
there is no
guaranteed life-saving way
to deal with an aggressive bear
some ploys
have proved more
successful than others.
Running's a poor choice.
Bear can outrun a racehorse.

Once you're face to face
speak softly. Take
off your pack
and set it down
to distract the grizzly.
Meanwhile back
slowly toward a large
sparsely-branched tree

but remember
black bears are agile climbers
in which case
a tree may not offer escape.

As a last resort you can
play dead. Drop
to the ground face down.
In this case
wearing your pack
may shield your body from attack.
Courage. Lie still. Sometimes
your bear may veer away.
If not
bears have been known
to inflict only minor injuries
upon the prone.

Is death
by bear to be preferred
to death by bomb? Under
these extenuating circumstances
your mind may make absurd
leaps. *The answer's yes.*
Come on in. Cherish
your wilderness.

I

In the Family

ATLANTIC CITY 1939

When I was young and returning from
death's door, I served as chaperone,
pale as waxworks, a holiday child,
under the bear laprobe in the back
of my courtesy uncle's Cadillac
careening through a world gone wild.

The Germans pushed into Poland. My
mother sat up front, close pressed
as bees to honey to Uncle Les
and wobbled the stick he shifted by.
I whooped my leftover cough but said
no word, a bear asleep or dead.

Later, in the Boardwalk arcade
when a chirping photographer made
me put my face in the hole with wings,
they snuggled behind him, winked and smiled
as he fussed and clicked the shutter's spring
and there I was corporeal
in the garb of the angel Gabriel,
forever a captive child.

Pink with ardor, not knowing why,
I longed for one of them to die

that slow September by the sea.
He fell on the beach at Normandy.
I never heard her say his name
again without a flush of shame
for my complicity.

THE CHAIN

My mother's insomnia over at last,
at dawn I enter her bureau drawers.
Under the petticoats, bedjackets, corsets,
under the unfinished knitting that crossed
continents with her, an affable animal,
I come on a hatbox of type-O any-hair,
heavy braids that have lain fifty years in this oval.
Between them, my mother's mother's calling card
engraved on brittle ivory vellum:
Mrs. Abraham Simon, Star Route 3, Radford.

Radford, Virginia, three thousand souls.
Here my mother spent her girlhood, not
without complications, playing
the Methodist church organ for weddings,
funerals, and the Sunday choir.
Here her mother, holding a lily-shaped
ear trumpet, stepped down from the surrey
Grandfather drove forty miles to Roanoke
to witness the blowing of the shofar
on Rosh Hashonah and Yom Kippur.

Affirming my past, our past in
a nation losing its memory, turning
its battlegrounds into parking lots,
slicking its regional differences over

with video games, substituting outer
space for history, I mourn
the type-O any-deaths of Mecca,
Athens, Babylon, Rome,
Radford, country towns
of middle-class hopes and tall corn.

Every year a new itinerant
piano teacher. New exercises
in the key of most-flats. 1908,
the first indoor toilet. The first
running hot water. My mother
takes weekly elocution lessons.
The radio, the telephone,
the Model T arrive. One by one
her sisters are sent north to cousins
in search of kindly Jewish husbands.

Surely having lived this long confers
a kind of aristocracy on my mother,
who kept to the end these talismans,
two dry links in the chain of daughters.
In the land of burley tobacco,
of mules in the narrow furrows,
in the land of diphtheria and strangles,
of revival meetings and stillborn angels,

in the land of eleven living siblings
I make my mother a dowager queen.

I give her back the chipped ruby goblets.
I hand over the battered Sheffield tureen
and the child I was, whose once-auburn hair
she scooped up like gems from the beauty-shop floor.

INTRODUCING THE FATHERS

For Anne Carpenter

Yours lugs shopping bags of sweet corn
via parlor car to enhance the lunches
of his fellow lawyers at the Century Club.
Sundays he sneaks from church to stretch a net
across the Nissequegue River
and catches shad as they swim up to spawn.

Mine locks up the store six nights at seven,
cracks coconuts apart on the brick hearth,
forces lobsters down in the boiling pot.
Sundays he lolls in silk pajamas,
and swaggers out at nightfall to play pinochle.

In our middle age we bring them back, these despots,
mine in shirtsleeves, yours in summer flannels,
whose war cry was: the best of everything!
and place them side by side, inflatable
Macy daddies ready for the big parade.

We open a friendship between them, sweetly posthumous,
and watch them bulge out twirling Malacca canes
into the simple future of straight losses,
still matching net worths, winning big at blackjack,
our golden warriors rising toward the Big Crash.

APPETITE

I eat these
wild red raspberries
still warm from the sun
and smelling faintly of jewelweed
in memory of my father

tucking the napkin
under his chin and bending
over an ironstone bowl
of the bright drupelets
awash in cream

my father
with the sigh of a man
who has seen all and been redeemed
said time after time
as he lifted his spoon

men kill for this.

SPREE

My father paces the upstairs hall
a large confined animal
neither wild nor yet domesticated.
About him hangs the smell of righteous wrath.
My mother is meekly seated
at the escritoire. Rosy from my bath
age eight-nine-ten by now I understand
his right to roar, hers to defy
the bill from Wanamaker's in his hand
the bill from Strawbridge's held high
the bill from Bonwit Teller
and the all plum-colored Blum Store.

His anger smells like dinner parties
like trays of frothy daiquiris.
Against the pre–World-War-Two prime
standing ribs his carving knife
flashes a little drunkenly. He charms
all the other Bonwit-bedecked wives
but something overripe malingers.
I wear his wide cigar bands on my fingers.

Oh God it is so noisy!
Under my bed a secret stair
a gold and purple escalator
takes me nightly down under the sea.

Such dancings, such carryings on
with the prince of this-or-that
with the duke of ne'er-do-well
I the plain one, a size too large to tell
grow tremulous at stickpin and cravat
I in toe shoes and tutu suddenly
see shopping is an art form
a kind of costume ball.

Papá, would we so humbly come
to the scene in the upstairs hall
on the first of every month, except
you chose the mice for footmen, clapped
to call up the coach and four?
You sent to Paris for the ermine muff
that says I'm rich. To think twelve poor
little things had their heads chopped off
to keep my hands unseemly warm!
When you went fishing down the well
for fox furs, hats with peacock plumes
velvet evening capes, what else befell?

You paid the bills, Papá. You cast the spell.

GRANDCHILD

For Yann

All night the *douanier* in his sentry box
at the end of the lane where France begins plays fox
and hounds with little spurts of cars
that sniff to a stop at the barrier
and declare themselves. I stand at the window
watching the ancient boundaries that flow
between my daughter's life and mine dissolve
like taffy pulled until it melts in half
without announcing any point of strain
and I am a young unsure mother again
stiffly clutching the twelve-limbed raw
creature that broke from between my legs, that stew
of bone and membrane loosely sewn up in
a fierce scared flailing other being.

We blink, two strangers in a foreign kitchen.
Now that you've drained your mother dry and will
not sleep, I take you in my arms, brimful
six days old, little feared-for mouse.
Last week when you were still a fish
in the interior, I dreamed you thus:
The *douanier* brought you curled up in his cap
buttoned and suited like him, authority's prop
—a good Victorian child's myth—
and in his other hand a large round cheese

ready to the point of runniness.
At least there, says the dream, no mysteries.

Toward dawn I open my daughter's cupboard on
a choice of calming teas—*infusions*—
verbena, fennel, linden, camomile,
shift you on my shoulder and fill the kettle.
Age has conferred on me a certain grace.
You're a package I can rock and ease
from wakefulness to sleep. This skill comes back
like learning how to swim. Comes warm and quick
as first milk in the breasts. I comfort you.
Body to body my monkey-wit soaks through.

Later, I wind the outside shutters up.
You sleep mouse-mild, topped with camomile.
Daylight slips past the *douane*. I rinse my cup.
My daughter troubles sleep a little while
longer. The just-milked cows across the way
come down their hillside single file
and the dream, the lefthand gift of ripened brie
recurs, smelly, natural, and good
wanting only to be brought true
in your own time: your childhood.

EXPATRIATE

Today from a paint-spattered ladder I pick the last
of the five thousand Kentucky Wonders that have embellished
the teepee with green pencils since you planted them in May,
you and the child, four pale seeds circling each pole.
In June you were still with us, although at arm's length always.
We watched hummingbirds suck sugar water from a bowl.

Today I am going up in the sky with these tendrils,
these snakelets that reach, reach, double back, and respell
ever ad astra the names of Bombay, Hong Kong, Singapore
and droplets of Indonesia called Sumba, Flores, Timor.

Sprung loose by the thrust of a beanstalk, victim
of wretched excess, of superabundance, today I am
going up to cross over and seize you, you and the little boy
who belong to us, although at arm's length always.
Down the broad green stem I will bear you home
in the numinous light of late summer to the brown loam.

A DISTANT GRANDCHILD
LISTENS TO FARM SOUNDS

He is waiting for Grandpa
to step out of the cassette.
The voice that sings him Old MacDonald
simply precedes the body
and so he waits as patiently
as the leopard-spotted dog
who barks on command and whacks
his tail against the woodbox.
Bumbling, gentle, with a big tongue
perhaps the dog will leap out too
after the song is sung.

In the barn the tape recorder
takes in the sound of horses nickering
as they wait for their measures of grain.
The lambs are easy to catch
aaahing in their greed. The aggie truck
that the child loved to ride in coughs
then sputters, playing the beautiful music
of old engines. When they went
to haul cordwood he sat up front.

He will ask to hear over and over
these sounds of Grandpa's devising.
The rain of his hammer, the scrape of his shovel,
the pitch of his whistle calling

the dog to his side, the horses from pasture.
The child has learned this language
while still awaiting his idol.
This is it, this nonappearance.
This is how gods are made.

CARING: A DREAM

Sepia the first part
the shuffle of the doomed
like an Indian documentary

a sprawl of dead elephants
and then outlined like a Rouault
greataunt Manya of the monkey

dirt under her fingernails
gray hairs flying out of her bun
and Beppo on her shoulder

comes back to me in primary colors
comes back noiselessly
in her electric car

straddling the center line
camps with hoboes along the Delaware
the shelf of her bosom swaddled in scarves

every wet tramp starved dog
mauled chipmunk Manya saved
deserved deserved

and especially Beppo of the scarred neck
the hapless organ grinder she rapped
on the head with an umbrella

then appeased with twenty dollars
Beppo who ate with her slept with her
combed her hair kissed her on the lips

deserved deserved O Manya
I want to tell you caring is small
susceptible fits in a pocket

nor is it one thing to save animals
and people another
but seamless

you who were no one's mother
come spraddle legged and sure
with monkey and funny car

framed in this dream
by the shuffle of the doomed
to command me to go on

II

Out There

SHOPPING IN FERNEY
WITH VOLTAIRE

Wearing a flowered nightgown
under his frockcoat, Voltaire
comes down the avenue of oaks
a basket on his arm. Looks
four ways at his poète-philosophe
likeness in the square
that vélomoteurs dive toward
careening off to either side
and walks into the crowd
of tidy Genevoises who swarm
each Saturday across the line
to stroll along the cobblestones
choosing among a hundred cheeses
sandbagged sausages
dripping Breton artichokes
oysters, olives, almonds, dates.

A little chitchat seems appropriate.
I ask him how he feels.
Fingering the fringy cornucopias
of black chanterelles
(les trompettes de la mort) he quotes
himself: qui veut voir une ombre?
I've read that in the Besterman
biography. Also about
the colic on demand.

Also the fainting fits
to dispatch hangers-on.

We rummage among the burly roots
fresh dug from local plots.
He chooses small white turnips
to tuck around the Sunday roast.
I tell him his remains
were exhumed thirteen years post-mortem.
Someone stole two teeth and his left foot.
He shrugs. —A useless passion,
necrophilia. About
that stupid recantation:
remember that I never took
communion! Let's be clear on that.
I told the Abbé, you will note
I'm spitting blood.
We must be careful not
to mingle mine with God's.
He grins. We stop at carts of citrus fruits
collect a dozen clementines
and pay with clanks of old-style coins.

One booth away
Amnesty International
has prisoners for sale.

Handbills cry aloud
the murdered, the disappeared,
the tortured, in before-
and-after photographs.
A self-improvement course
run riot in reverse.
Anyone who cares to can
adopt a prisoner of conscience.
Voltaire's list is longer than
old-school homework Latin scansions.

In my day—he sighs
reliving the stench of pain
—torture was a public act.
Before they killed a man
they broke him on the rack.
The main thing was to die
courageously. It's different now.
No longer personal.
His sharp fox face so like
Max Adrian's Pangloss
as if he had just caught
out of the corner of his eye
the murderings en masse.
The nuclear juggernaut.
The Great Beast lumbering past.

The labor camps, the stripping off
of civilization's mask.

We walk together toward
the border at Meyrin.
The sky goes yellow as
old corn shucks. Rain will drench
the ancient hills, thorn-fenced,
these stubbled fields, the cows
kneeling along the ridge.
Behind us, Ferney brims with light.
—Adieu, he says. —Take my advice.
Always live close to the edge
so that when sudden flight
is called for, you can put
a foot down on the other side.
We embrace three times, à la suisse.
I cross the *douane*, then turn
to watch the old philosopher
mushrooms, roots, and tangerines in hand
limp back to the Enlightenment
and disappear.

AT A PRIVATE SHOWING
IN 1982

For Gillian Anderson

This loving attention to the details:
faces by Bosch and Bruegel,
the mélange of torture tools,
the carpentry of the stake,
the Catherine wheel,
the bars, spires, gibbets, pikes—
I confess my heart sank
when they brought out the second reel . . .

Anorectic Jeanne d'Arc,
how long it takes her
to burn to death in this picture!
When monks fast, it is called ascetic.
The film beamed on the dining-room wall
of an old brownstone
undergoing gentrification on Capitol Hill,
glass shards and daffodils
on alternate lawns,
harpsichord, bare board table,
cheese, nuts, jug wine,

and striding across the screen,
hauntingly young, unbowed,
not yet absurd, not yet insane,
Antonin Artaud in a bit part:
the "good" priest,

the one who declaims
"You are persecuting a saint!"
but does not offer
to die beside her.

And how is any of this
different today,
except now in color, and talky—
this prurient close
examination of pain,
fanaticism, terror?

Though the judges dress
like World War I British
soldiers in tin helmets
and Sam Browne belts,
though the music exactly
matches the mouthed words,
though Jeanne's
enormous wounded-doe's eyes
roll up or shut down
in hope, in anguish,
though Renée Falconetti,
who plays this part, was merely
a comic-stage actress
and never shows up on celluloid again,

though Artaud
tonsured for the set
walks the streets of Paris
in costume in 1928
and is mocked by urchins
and is peppered with catcalls,
what does it profit us?

Artaud will die in the madhouse
in terror for his immortal soul,
Falconetti will drop out of sight,
an émigrée in the Argentine,
we few will finish the wine
and skulk out on this spring night
together, unsafe on Capitol Hill.

MAKING HISTORY IN FLORIDA

Atlantic Center for the Arts

"First half moon after
my birthday. Left four flowered
Japanese napkin
rings in the cupboard,"
Allen Ginsberg
wrote on the wall inside
the bedroom closet
of this cottage
in a quavering, large,
childishly rounded hand.
Dated his entry,
added his age, and
noted it was 10:55 p.m.
Om.

Ferlinghetti,
his surname printed
in block letters,
was here, too. Omitted
the Lawrence.
Under, in a perfectly
serene script, Julie
Elizabeth Ferlinghetti.
Mary Lee Settle
George Garrett
Audre Lorde

chastely contributed
to the scorecard
signing just their names
and dates of tenure.

O Kilroy, only you
are absent
wherever you are,
and the little face
the artist used to add,
fat nose
drooping over a fence.
But that
was in the forties
when it said
a homesick GI
had visited the place.
That was during
the last war that made sense.

THE POET VISITS EGYPT
AND ISRAEL

Sand, sand. In the university the halls,
seats, table tops, sills, are gritty with it.
Birds fly in and out at the open windows.
During the lecture an elderly porter
splendid in turban and djellaba,
shuffles in, opens a cabinet on the apron,
plugs in a microphone, spits into it twice,
and plumps it down on the lectern.
She continues to speak, amplified,

on American women poets since World War One
to an audience familiar with Dickinson,
Poe, and at a safe remove, Walt Whitman.
Afterward, thick coffee in thimbles. Sticky cakes
with the faculty. In this polite fortress
a floating unease causes her hands to shake
although nothing is said that could trespass
on her status as guest from another, unveiled, life.
She is a goddess, rich, white, American,

and a Jew. It says so in some of her poems.
There are no visible Jews in the American
Embassy, nor at the Cultural Center, and none
turns up in Cairo or Alexandria
although an itinerant rabbi is rumored
to cross from the other side once a fortnight

and serve the remaining congregants. The one
synagogue, a beige stucco Parthenon,
sleeps in the Sabbath sun, shuttered tight
and guarded by languid soldiers with bayonets.

All that she cannot say aloud she holds
hostage in her head: the congruities
of bayonets and whips; starved donkeys
and skeletal horses pulling impossible loads;
the small, indomitable Egyptian flies
that perch on lips, settle around the eyes
and will not be waved away. Like traffic
in Cairo, they persist, closing the margin
between life and death to a line so thin

as to become imperceptible.
Transported between lectures, she is tuned
to the rich variety of auto horns, each one
shriller, more cacophonous, peremptory
than its abutter. The decibel level
means everyone drives with windows closed,
tapedeck on full, airconditioning at maximum.
Thus conveyed, fender nudging fender,
she comes to ancient Heliopolis

where the Sheraton sits apart in an oasis.
Gaudier than Las Vegas, she thinks, checking in.

Behind her in the lobby, two BMWs,
several sheiks, exotic birds in cages,
and plumbing fixtures of alabaster
ornament this nouveau riche heaven.
Backlighted to enhance their translucency,
the toilet tank and bidet bowl are radiant,
the kind of kitsch she wishes she didn't notice.

Outdoors in the sports enclave, pool attendants
in monogrammed turtlenecks, like prep-school athletes,
carry iced salvers from bar to umbrellaed table,
proffer thick towels, reposition chaises longues
for the oiled, bikini-ed, all-but-naked bodies
of salesmen's wives and hostesses on holdover.
What do they think about, the poet wonders,
as they glide among the infidels, these men
whose own wives wrap up head to toe in public,

whose cousins' cousins creep from day to day
in a state of chronic lowgrade emergency.
Anonymous again in transit,
the poet leaves for Tel Aviv at night.
She watches a pride of pregnant tabbies stalk
cockroaches in the threadbare airport lounge
for protein enough to give a litter suck.

Always the Saving Remnant learns to scrounge
to stay alive. Could she now name the ten

plagues God sent? Uneasy truce exists
between these two antagonists.
El Al's flight, a frail umbilicus
that loops three times a week to the Holy Land,
is never posted on the Departures Board.
Security's intense. Shepherded
by an Israeli packing two guns,
she's bused with a poor handful to the tarmac.
The takeoff's dodgy, as if in fear of flak,

as if God might turn aside and harden
Pharaoh's heart, again fill up the sea.
Once down, she knows the desert by its gardens,
the beachfront by its senior citizens
assembled for calisthenics on the sand.
An hour later in the Old City
she sees a dozen small white donkeys,
descendants of the one that Jesus straddled,
trot docilely beside Volkswagen Beetles,

Mercedes cabs, tour buses full of young
camera-strapped, light-metered Japanese.
She peers into archaeological digs that reach

down through limestone to the days of Babylon,
pridefully down to the first tribes of Yahweh
sacrificing scapegoats on a stone.
Down through the rubble of bones and matter
—Constantinian, Herodian, Hasmonean—
that hold up the contemporary clutter.

At the Western Wall, Sephardic Jews,
their genders separated by a grill,
clap for the bar mitzvah boy with spit curls
who struggles to lift a gold-encrusted Torah
that proclaims today he is a man.
The poet polkas, dancing to tambourine
and bongo drums with other passersby.
Behind her, dinosaurs against the sky,
two Hapag-Lloyd Ltd. cranes

raise massive stacks of facing stones,
the eighth or ninth or tenth civilization
to go up on the same fought-over bedrock.
Near the Via Dolorosa, among the schlock
for sale—amber beads, prayer rugs, camel saddles—
lamb legs are offered, always with one testicle
attached. Ubiquitous sweet figs, olive trees
botanically certified to be
sprouts from the sacred roots of Gethsemane.

She tries to haggle for a sheepskin coat
but lacks the swagger needed for cheerful insult.
A man whose concentration-camp tattoo
announces he was zero six nine eight
picks through a tangle of ripe kumquats
beside a Bedouin, her hands and face daubed blue,
who could as easily have been a Druid,
the poet thinks, and she an early Christian.
In a restored Burnt House from 70 A.D.,

the year the Romans sacked the second Temple,
she dutifully clambers down to view
scorch marks, gouged walls, some human bones, amid
a troop of new recruits in green fatigues.
Girls the shape and gawk of girls back home.
Boys whose bony wrists have overshot
their cuffs already. Not yet on alert
but destined to serve on one front or another,
eye contact in this shrine says: Jews together.

Meanwhile, clusters of Hasidic zealots
(most of them recent Brooklyn imports)
in bobbing dreadlocks and black stovepipe hats
pedal breakneck along the claustral streets
of the Arab Quarter on ten-speed bikes to await
the messianic moment any minute

now. Look for a pillar of fire and in it
the one true Blessed-be-He, whose very name
cannot be spoken in the waiting game.

The one true Blessed-be-He, who still is hidden.
The poet sees a film on television,
news clips of shock troops: Syrian women
soldiers holding live snakes, biting them
on command, chewing and spitting out
the raw flesh. *In this way we will chew
and spit out the enemy.* Guess who.
Parental discretion was advised for viewing.
As if the young in these geographies

had not yet heard of torture, frag bombs, the crying
out at night that is silenced by garrote.
Another clip, the commentator said,
closeups of Assad's crack soldiers ordered
to strangle puppies and squeeze out blood
to drink as he reviewed the troops, was censored.
Judged too depraved for any audience.
How much is propaganda, how
much real? How did we get here,

the poet wonders, in the name of God,
in the name of all gods revving up their motors

to this high-pitched hum, like tripwire
stretched taut before the spark ignites the fuse
fragmenting life for life, blood running
in the dust to mingle Shiite, Druse,
Israeli, French, American.
If I forget thee, O Jerusalem,
may my right hand forget its cunning.

IN THE ABSENCE OF BLISS

Museum of the Diaspora, Tel Aviv

The roasting alive of rabbis
in the ardor of the Crusades
went unremarked in *Europe from*
the Holy Roman Empire to 1918,
open without prerequisite
when I was an undergraduate.

While reciting the Sh'ma in full
expectation that their souls
would waft up to the bosom
of the Almighty the rabbis burned,
pious past the humming extremes
of pain. And their loved ones with them.
Whole communities tortured and set aflame
in Christ's name
while chanting Hear, O Israel.

Why?
Why couldn't the rabbis recant,
kiss the Cross, pretend?
Is God so simple that He can't
sort out real from sham?
Did He want
these fanatic autos-da-fé, admire
the eyeballs popping,
the corpses shrinking in the fire?

We live in an orderly
universe of discoverable laws,
writes an intelligent alumna
in *Harvard Magazine*.
Bliss is belief,
agnostics always say
a little condescendingly
as befits mandarins who function
on a higher moral plane.

Consider our contemporary
Muslim kamikazes
hurling their explosives-
packed trucks through barriers.
Isn't it all the same?
They too die cherishing the fond
certitude of a better life beyond.

We walk away from twenty-two
graphic centuries of kill-the-jew
and hail, of all things, a Mercedes
taxi. The driver is Yemeni,
loves rock music and hangs
each son's picture—three so far—
on tassels from his rearview mirror.

I do not tell him that in Yemen
Jewish men, like women, were forbidden
to ride their donkeys astride,
having just seen this humiliation
illustrated on the Museum screen.

When his parents came
to the Promised Land, they entered
the belly of an enormous
silver bird, not knowing whether
they would live or die.
No matter. As it was written,
the Messiah had drawn nigh.

I do not ask, who tied
the leaping ram inside the thicket?
Who polished, then blighted the apple?
Who loosed pigs in the Temple,
set tribe against tribe
and nailed man in His pocket?

But ask myself, what would
I die for and reciting what?
Not for Yahweh, Allah, Christ,
those patriarchal fists
in the face. But would

I die to save a child?
Rescue my lover? Would
I run into the fiery barn
to release animals,
singed and panicked, from their stalls?

Bliss is belief, but where's
the higher moral plane I roost on?
This narrow plank given to splinters.
No answers. Only questions.

GLADLY

When the whale washed ashore on Billingsgate Shoal
where was I but beached at the farthest end of the map
casting off ballpoint pens gone pale
ripping the Latin words from legal pads.

While the town put out to sea in dories of green
red blue or elephant gray where was I but noisily going
gray as the whale itself. There they were rowing
rowing up to the anterior fin, anchoring fast

climbing aboard as if en route to Oak Bluffs,
as if on the old Bourne Bridge, as if
that barnacled quivering slab were
God's own tractor tire He chose to puncture.

I who was weeks getting back to my shoal
by way of small towns missed out on walking the whale
the length of a regulation swimming pool
missed out on the stench that set in, on the Coast Guard

all buckled and businesslike towing the poor
dead Jonah-house southerly past the bar
so it could most reverently be deep-sixed.
Cousin, Mama, you were on my barefoot lifelist.

How else to know our common root but through you
who are compost now on the Atlantic shelf?
I who was absent oh yes knees buckling from
the touch would have gladly walked you myself.

WAITING FOR THE END IN NEW SMYRNA BEACH, FLORIDA

At the corner of Lytle
and South Dixie Freeway a pale
young woman, baby on one arm, crooks
in the other a placard that asks
WHERE WILL YOU SPEND ETERNITY?
while the husband, hearty, even beefy
waves all to COME TO JESUS
and behind them on the grass
two sallow little girls fight
over a ragdoll. From time to time it
rains. They stand foursquare
sheltered in the Lord, pinning car
by car its occupants
en route to surf or Sunday brunch
with eye contact as steadfast as
an egret grazing the canals
who darts and pecks and lunges
and after an eternity
at Lytle and South Dixie
the light changes.

VISITING PROFESSOR

At MIT on the oval
my students stretch out like corpses
this day of budded maples.
Like the dead of Beirut in the sun.

Here everything is hopeful
because unconsidered. Fierce in
their indolence my students
turn themselves over sunning.

This evening under fluorescent lights
in a cooling classroom we will discuss
poems of the apocalypse
which serenely never happens

in their dreams. In mine, that one
Poseidon submarine carrying
like the fish, its eggs enough
to flood the pond, warheads enough

to level every medium
every large city in
the Soviet Union, that one
Poseidon sub sticks up its snub nose.

Diogenes at ninety held his breath
until he suffocated, so goes the myth
that says how much we want to be in charge.
My students will colonize

outer space. They will
domesticate the solar cell.
Syzygy and the molecular
cloning of genes will not overpower

their odes to the 21st century
their love poems and elegies.
Meanwhile their illegal puppies
wrestle among them on the oval

in springtime in Cambridge again
in a world where all, all is possible.
The chrome of new dandelions
assaults the sun.

LOUISE BOURGEOIS EXHIBIT

Museum of Modern Art 1983

This is no place for Renoir's little girls
or their rapturous mothers. Interiors here
—however grotesque, they are perfectly tidy—
beckon or seize suggesting ways
we are held male and female, pinned inside
or beneath. And yet we assume she painted
her share of apples and pears highlighted
on velvet before taking up picket fences
stones and pillars, toothy vaginas
roomsful of phalluses.

In the photograph on the frontispiece
of the Museum's brochure we have
her likeness wrapped in something feathery:
kind face worked in little rivulets
old-fashioned hairdo pulled back with waves
at the temples. She looks like everyone's
oldest, wisest, happiest and most untrammeled
auntie going her own way crumbling
graham crackers in bed

getting up to paint, pace, sculpt, pour latex
at three in the morning, carving body parts
bubbles and blisters, pods, poles
bulges of life force, nests and lairs
to contain them. In marble or wood

plaster or rubber she makes sweet clusters
of penises wearing hats, fat clumps
of breasts pillowed like clouds
or torpedoes.

Wherever we look things stand up
register one another's width and breadth.
Bourgeois announces *I am not*
particularly aware of the erotic
in my art. She tells the world *This is*
my statement of refusal to death.

VIDEO CUISINE

They are weighing the babies again on color television.
They are hanging these small bags of bones up in canvas slings
to determine which ones will receive the dried-milk mush,
the concentrate made out of ground-up trash fish.

For years we have watched them, back-lit by the desert,
these miles of dusty hands holding out goatskins or cups,
their animals dead or dying of rinderpest,
and after the credits come up I continue to sit

through Dinner with Julia, where, in a French fish
poacher big enough for a small brown baby, an
Alaska salmon simmers in a court bouillon.
For a first course, steak tartare to awaken the palate.

With it Julia suggests a zinfandel. This scene
has a polite, a touristy flavor to it,
and I let it play. But somewhere Oxfam goes on
spooning gluey gruel between the parched lips

of potbellied children, the ones who perhaps can be saved
from kwashiorkor—an ancient Ghanaian word—
though with probable lowered IQs, the voiceover explains,
caused by protein deficiencies linked to the drought

and the drought has grown worse with the gradual increase in
    herds
overgrazing the thin forage grasses of the Sahel.
This, says the voice, can be laid to the natural greed
of the nomad deceived by technicians digging new wells

which means (a slow pan of the sand) that the water table has
    dropped.
And now to Julia's table is borne the resplendent fish.
Always the camera is angled so that the guests look up.
Among them I glimpse that sly Dean, Jonathan Swift.

After the credits come up I continue to sit
with those who are starving to death in a distant nation
squatting, back-lit by the desert, hands out, in my head
and the Dublin Dean squats there too, observing the population

that waits for too little dried milk, white rice, trash fish.
Always the camera is angled so they look up
while their babies are weighed in slings on color television,
look into our living rooms and the shaded rooms we sleep in.

HOW TO SURVIVE
NUCLEAR WAR

After reading Ibuse's Black Rain

Brought low in Kyoto,
too sick with chills and fever
to take the bullet train to Hiroshima,
I am jolted out of this geography,
pursued by Nazis, kidnapped, stranded
when the dam bursts, my life
always in someone else's hands.
Room service brings me tea and aspirin.

This week the Holy Radish
Festival, pure white daikons
one foot long grace all the city's shrines.
Earlier, a celebration for the souls
of insects farmers may have trampled on
while bringing in the harvest.
Now shall I repent?
I kill to keep whatever
pleases me. Last summer
to save the raspberries
I immolated hundreds of coppery
Japanese beetles.

In some respects,
Ibuse tells me,
radiation sickness is less
terrible than cancer. The hair

comes out in patches. Teeth
break off like matchsticks
at the gum line but the loss
is painless. Burned skin itches,
peels away in strips.
Everywhere the black rain fell
it stains the flesh like a tattoo
but weeks later, when
survivors must expel
day by day in little pisses
the membrane lining the bladder
pain becomes an extreme grammar.

I understand we did this.
I understand
we may do this again
before it is done to us.
In case it is thought of
to do to us.

Just now, the homage that
I could not pay the irradiated dead
gives rise to a dream.
In it, a festival to mourn
the ritual maiming of the ginkgo,
pollarding that lops

all natural growth
from the tumorous stump
years of pruning creates.
I note that these faggots
are burned. I observe that the smoke
is swallowed with great ceremony.
Thereupon every severed shoot
comes back, takes on
a human form, fan-shaped,
ancient, all-knowing,
tattered like us.

This means
we are all to be rescued.

Though we eat animals
and wear their skins,
though we crack mountains
and insert rockets in them

this signifies
we will burn and go up.
We will be burned and come back.

I wake naked, parched,
my skin striped by sunlight.

Under my window
a line of old ginkgos hunkers down.
The new sprouts that break from
their armless shoulders are
the enemies of despair.

III

On the Farm

GETTING THROUGH

I want to apologize
for all the snow falling in
this poem so early in the season.
Falling on the calendar of bad news.
Already we have had snow lucid,
snow surprising, snow bees
and lambswool snow. Already
snows of exaltation have covered
some scars. Larks and the likes
of paisleys went up. But lately the sky
is letting down large-print flakes
of old age. Loving this poor place,
wanting to stay on, we have endured
an elegiac snow of whitest jade,
subdued biographical snows
and public storms, official and profuse.

Even if the world is ending
you can tell it's February
by the architecture of the pastures.
Snow falls on the pregnant mares,
is followed by a thaw, and then
refreezes so that everywhere
their hill upheaves into a glass mountain.
The horses skid, stiff-legged, correct
position, break through the crust

and stand around disconsolate
lipping wisps of hay.
Animals are said to be soulless.
Unable to anticipate.

No mail today.
No newspapers. The phone's dead.
Bombs and grenades, the newly disappeared,
a kidnapped ear, go unrecorded
but the foals flutter inside
warm wet bags that carry them
eleven months in the dark.
It seems they lie transversely, thick
as logs. The outcome is well known.
If there's an April
in the last frail snow of April
they will knock hard to be born.

SUNDAYS IN MARCH

For Celeste and Robert Klein

Our bear, we call him now.
Ursus minor, pure in his hole
betrayed by yellow snow
and a melted patch of scat
around the ash tree's bole.
Likely ousted just last fall
to make way for the new crop.
Denned up all winter on your scarp
he's come out periodically,
taken three steps to pee,
gone up the canted trunk
and stretched, like a basketball dunker.
Higher claw marks every week
attest to his improved physique.

In order to lean in and touch
his black moth-eaten laprobe fur,
in order to feel his lean flanks twitch
under our palms, we four vigil-keepers
each Sunday climbed a slope so steep
we seized handholds on saplings to
underwrite our view.
We whispered over him as if
his trance were sacred to this cliff.
As if these watchdays might compare

with other vigils of our lives—
the sixties' civil rights sit-ins.
The lyings down against the war.
Peacewalks to halt the bomb. Believe
me, bear's the merest rung we've
stepped on climbing Jacob's ladder.

Now let us live in harmony
with every breathing thing,
the church exhales. Our horse manure
beds your garden, half your pig's
in our freezer. The children,
all grown and scattered, cross
time zones now and then to visit,
victims of the oldest feelings
that nothing changes, everything is broken.
So be it. For years we've lugged
back and forth the same unopened jug
of sour red Chianti, token
that we're each other's home-and-home.

Earlier today we bought
four market lambs to fatten
and dress out next November,
held them up, floppy as pillow ticks,

for the elastrator
and stayed to smile at two bummers,
orphans high on their four-hour fix
of milk replacer, skidding among
the kitchen chairs with the farmer's mongrel.
Outside, the laying hens no longer
laying will have their necks wrung.
Everything pays for growing tame,
whatever you call it. Our forebears,
those good gray Victorians,
caged wild birds and blinded them
with hot needles. It was thought
that this would make them sing.
We castrate what we plan to eat
to purge the musk from the meat.
He made their glowing colors
He made their tiny wings.

We settle our accounts and go,
the four of us clumsier now
plodding through rotten snow,
rising toward our bear
to put the wildness back in.
Each pilgrimage we make
I hope to find our avatar

cranky, thin, waked
by the calendar,
vanished from the body of the tree.
Today, at last. Something we watched,
touched, and let be.

STRUT

Every morning to guard against glut I chop
zucchini zealots for the lambs
who are not particularly grateful.
They prefer old apples and fresh grain.

Every morning I rethink how common green
—pond scum, a thousand sumac sprouts
brome and rye grass, birdsfoot trefoil
milkweed, poke, dock, dill, sorrel

bush and shrub, soft and hardwoods, all
leafy headed—must go down again in
frost and come again. Is this a deep
head-tilting meditative thought, or

vernal instinctual, nothing more?
Here come the marbleized rat-wet new foals
blowing blue bubbles like divers into air
on their feet in minutes finding

the mares' teats by trial-and-error blind
butting stagger-dance. And here comes
cakewalk cocky with the whole mess
of birth and rebirth the strut of the season.

Almost bliss.

IN THE UPPER PASTURE

In the evergreen grove that abuts the pasture we are
limbing low branches, carting away deadwood,
cutting close to the trunk so the sap does not bleed,
to make a shelter, a run-in for foals and their mares.
We will not shorten the lives of these hemlocks and pines
in the afternoon of our own lives, yet I am sad
to think that the dell will outlast us and our bloodlines.

Is this a pastoral? Be not deceived
by the bellows of leathery teats giving suck,
by the fringe of delicate beard that pricks
its braille notes on the muzzle of the newborn.
When instinct whinnies between dam and foal
at night in the rain, do not be lulled.
Each of us whimpers his way through the forest alone.

With scrap lumber we patiently fence off
a triad of trees that have grown so close to each other
a young horse darting through might be taken prisoner.
Let the babies be safe here, let them lie down on pine duff
away from the merciless blackflies, out of the weather.
Under the latticework of old trees let me stand
pitch-streaked and pleasured by this small thing we have done.

OUT IN IT

Crouched under my desk, at a bad clap
eighty pounds of spotted dog quakes.
I too lose my head in a storm like this
or would like at least to bury it.
Each time the white knife slashes
the barn cats tunnel deeper into hay.
The horses wheel and gallop while
cymbals clash overhead. They do not know
what trouble they're in wearing
their iron shoes out there in the pasture
when the serpent's tongue darts down
to lick salt from the earth. Last year
one hundred and some-odd people died
in the USA, seized where they stood
under old trees at the edge of the eighteenth tee
or racing out back to snatch bedsheets
off the line.
                But these are small shocks,
these pyrotechnics, Hephaestus twiddling his thumbs.
Do not ask me to feel too much here at the fulcrum!

Inside me a whole city
a flagdraped nation
of down vests and LL Bean boots
a great big grapefruit

of a planet that is 70% ocean
and 25,000 miles around
is waiting. Where do we want
to be when the first strike comes?
Out in it with all our kith and kin
crisping in one another's arms.

DIARY

Mid-April: out of sync
their separate baaings float
up from the pasture to pluck
at the bedclothes all night.
Sleepless together
all of us missing our mothers.

Soon they assemble for grain
dashed into the flat black pan,
come up to the gate of the pen
and huddle like football players
asking, what are fingers?
What's in a hand?

We bring them our apple peels.
Pull them choice clover, vetch.
The littlest sits in my lap.
Somebody's child once had a sheep
on wheels, bedecked
I now understand, with dead fleece.

Four fat white blobs
darting like protein spots in reverse
over the granite outcroppings.
Everything mica-flecked

in sunlight! For contrast
spikes of Indian paintbrush.

We will eat them.
Resolutely I will not name them:
littlest one with the face of a mouse,
almost as small, appaloosa-spotted.
Rabbit-eared number 3.
Wide One, dingy white eunuch.

September nights they return to the fold
to lie layered like petals.
Cicadas tick, bats swoop low.
Four more weeks in the meadow.
More grain to prepare them
like Hansel and Gretel.

November. Thank you, lambs
for your thousands of raisin
droppings early and late
dotting the land with nitrogen.
We meant you no harm
but this. Forgive our full plates.

MY ELUSIVE GUEST

Thoreau loved the grayness of them, homespun
with leafy horns like lichen made of bone.
God's own horses, poor timid creatures, he said
in 1846 in THE MAINE WOODS
and then went on to wonder why they stood
so high at the shoulders, why so long a head,
no tail to speak of. *How like the camelopard,*
he said, rolling the archaic word
on his tongue: *high before and low behind*
and stayed admiring them, upwind.

A hundred years later, the widow Blau
whose rockbound farm I now inhabit
broomed a moose out of her kitchen garden
thinking it the neighbor's brown cow
marauding among the vegetables at dawn
then looked up to behold those rabbit
ears, that wet nearsighted eye
that ferny rack of gray on a still-gray sky

and none since. Spring mornings at first light
sometimes through fog some heavy weight
shifts and wavers against the line of trees
and wanting it in my blood, like a spray
of musk, I beckon the elusive guest,
willing it close. My wild thing, my moose.

A NEW ENGLAND GARDENER
GETS PERSONAL

Kale
curls. Laughs at cold rain.
Survives
leaf-snapping hail.
Under snow, stays green.
Comes crisp as a handclap
to the bowl,
then lies meekly down
with lettuces and cole.

Willynilly
after years of no-peppers
a glut of them
perfect as Peter Piper's.
Only piccalilli
will get shut of them.
None grow riper
none redden in this clime
but such sublime
pectorals! Such green hips!
No Greek torso could be
more nobly equipped.

What ails you, cherry tomato?
Why do you blossom and never bear?
Is it acid rain you're prey to
or nicotine in the air?

Are you determinate or not,
wanting trellises,
strings to cling to from the pot?
What evil spell is this?

Apple on a stalk
kohlrabi
grows fronds in its ears.
Stands stiff as a bobby
when the Queen appears.
Quoth she: my dears,
eat this pale knob when small
or not at all.

Winters, like money in the bank,
that dull gargantuan, the swede,
yellow, thick, and faintly rank,
is eaten by cattle and people in need.

Carrot
wants company in bed.
Presses
to be held on either side
by purslane, chickweed
and coarser grasses.
Meanwhile puts down deep alone
its secret orange cone.

SHELLING JACOBS
CATTLE BEANS

All summer
they grew unseen
in the corn patch
planted to climb on Silver Queen
Butter and Sugar
compete with witch
grass and lamb's-quarters
only to stand naked, old crones,
Mayan, Macedonian
sticks of antiquity
drying alone
after the corn is taken.

I, whose ancestors
put on sackcloth and ashes
for the destruction of the Temple
sit winnowing the beans
on Rosh Hashanah
in the September sun
of New Hampshire.
Each its own example:
a rare bird's egg
cranberry- or blood-flecked
as cool in the hand
as a beach stone
no two exactly alike

yet close as snowflakes.
Each pops out of the dry
husk, the oblong shaft
that held it,
every compartment a tight fit.

I sit on the front stoop
a romantic, thinking
what a centerpiece!
not, what a soup!
layering beans into
their storage jars.
At Pompeii the food
ossified on the table
under strata of ash.
Before that, the Hebrews
stacked bricks
under the Egyptian lash.

Today
in the slums of Lebanon
Semite is set against Semite
with Old Testament fervor.
Bombs go off in Paris,
Damascus, New York,
a network of retaliations.

Where is the God of
my fathers, that I
may pluck Him out of the lineup?
That I may hand back my ticket?

In case we outlast
the winter, in case
when the end comes
ending all matter,
the least gravel
of Jacobs Cattle remain,
let me shell out the lot.
Let me put my faith in the bean.

AFTER THE HARVEST

Pulling the garden I always think
of starving to death, of how it would be to get by
on what the hard frost left untouched
at the end of the world: a penance of kale,
jerusalem artichokes, brussels sprouts,
some serviceberries, windfall apples
and the dubious bounty of hickory nuts.

Pretty slim pickings for the Tribulation
if that's what this is, preceding
the Rapture I choose to be left out of.
Having never acceded to an initial coming
I hold out no hope for a second
let alone this bland vision of mail-order angels
lifting born-again drivers up from behind the wheel
leaving the rest of us loose on the highways
to play out a rudderless dodgem.

When parents were gods survival was a game
I played in my head, reading by flashlight
under the covers *Swiss Family Robinson*
and *The Adventures of Perrine,* who lived in a hut
and was happy weaving moccasins out of marsh grass.

I longed to be orphaned like her, out on my own,
befriending little creatures of the woods,

never cold or wet or hungry. To be snug
in spite of the world's world is the child-hermit's plan.
Meekly I ate the detested liver and lima beans.

Now all of the gods agree, no part of the main
can survive the nuclear night. And yet,
like a student of mine who is writing a book
on an island linked by once-a-week ferry
to Juneau, where one pay phone and a hot spring bath
suffice for all, in innocent ways we still
need to test the fringe of the freezing dark.
He thinks he can be happy there year round
and the child in me envies his Cave of the Winds.

Meanwhile I fling cornstalks and cucumber,
pea and squash vines across the fence
and the horses mosey over to beg carrot tops.
I am mesmerized by the gesture, handfeeding
feathery greens to the broodmares. This could

be last year or five years or ten years ago
and I sense it is ending, this cycle of saving
and sprouting: a houseful of seedlings in March,
the cutworms of May, June's ubiquitous weeds,
the long August drought peppered with grasshoppers

even as I lop the last purple cabbage, big
as a baby's head, big as my grandson's brain
who on the other side of the world is naming
a surfeit of tropical fruits in five-tone Thai.
A child I long to see again,
growing up in a land where thousands, displaced,
unwanted, diseased, are awash in despair.

Who will put the wafer of survival on their tongues,
lift them out of the camps, restore
their villages, replant their fields, those gardens
that want to bear twelve months of the year?
Who gets Rapture?

Sidelong we catch film clips of the Tribulation
but nobody wants to measure the breadth and length
of the firestorms that lurk in Overkill,
certitude of result through overwhelming strength,
they define it in military circles,

their flyboys swirling up in sunset contrails.
The local kids suit up to bob for apples,
go trick-or-treating on both sides of Main.
November rattles its dry husks down the food chain
on this peaceable island at the top of the hill.

THE LONG APPROACH

In the eel-thin belly of the Metro Swearingen
banking in late afternoon over Boston Harbor,
the islands eleven lily pads, my life loose as a frog's,
I try to decipher the meaning of hope rising up again
making music in me all the way from Scranton
where the slag heaps stand like sentries shot dead
at their posts. Hope rising up in my Saab hatchback,
one hundred thousand honest miles on it as I speed
due north from LaBell's cut-rate autopark
to my spiny hillside farm in New Hampshire.

March 21st. Snow still frosts the manure heap
and flurries lace the horses' ample rumps
but in here it's Stephen Foster coming back to me
unexpurgated, guileless, all by heart.
'Tis summer, the darkies are gay, we sang in Miss Dupree's
fifth grade in a suburb that I fled long ago.
Gone are my friends from the cotton fields away
to—an allusion that escaped me—a better land I know.
O the melancholia as I too longed to depart.
Now I belt out Massa's in de cold cold ground
and all the darkies are a'weepin on route I-93
but what I think of are the french-pastel mornings
daylit at five in my own hills in June when I may
leap up naked, happy, with no more premonition

than the mother of the Pope had. How the same
old pump of joy restarts for me, going home!

What I understand from travel is how luck
hangs in the lefthand lane fifteen miles
over the limit and no cop, no drunk, no ice slick.
Only the lightweight ghosts of racist lyrics
soaring from my throat in common time.
Last week leaving Orlando in a steep climb
my seatmate told me flying horses must be loaded
facing the tail of the plane so they may brace
themselves at takeoff. Otherwise you run
the risk they'll panic, pitch over backwards,
smash their hocks. Landing, said the groom,
there is little we can do for them except
pray for calm winds and ask the pilot
to make a long approach.

O brace me, my groom. Pray for calm winds.
Carry me back safely where the snow stands deep in March.
I'm going home the old way with a light hand on the reins
making the long approach.